FUN WAYS TO BEING ALONE

A guide to a Satisfying life of Happiness in Solitude

By

Walter Nzeh

COPY RIGHTS

TABLE OF CONTENTS

INTRODUCTION

If you're someone who thrives on the company of people, alone time may often seem tough to genuinely appreciate. But being alone is a normal part of the human experience; we'll all be alone at least once, whether by choice or by fate.

Moreover, our connection with ourselves is the only one we're guaranteed to have for the remainder of our lives—and so it's worth maintaining it so we're able to enjoy our own company as much as we do that of our friends and lovers. Ahead, we dig into the psychology of being happy alone and advice from experts on how to get there.

CHAPTER 1

« THE PSYCHOLOGY OF BEING HAPPY ALONE.

All individuals demand some amount of alone time. It's when we are alone that we're able to completely hear our thoughts and emotions, absorb the events and experiences from the day, and evaluate our present needs and care for them. Alone time allows us the opportunity to determine what is our own, independent from what is coming from our surroundings and others.

This self-awareness and self-tending are crucial to our everyday functioning, as being detached from our own emotions and needs frequently come at the expense of our health and well-being. It's how individuals may spend months being weary and stressed at work before understanding they're suffering from burnout or how a person in a toxic relationship would repeatedly disregard their own needs in search of pleasing a partner who's not healthy for them. It's why therapists believe even the healthiest couples need alone time apart from one other.

According to a psychologist, certain individuals may be more prone to liking alone. "Personality traits, such as a predisposition toward extroversion, may undoubtedly contribute to a person's capacity to feel pleased while they're alone," she says, "That is, those strong in extroversion (one of the so-called "Big Five personality qualities") may be more prone to suffer with alone time than introverts.

That said, being able to appreciate being alone is a talent that all individuals benefit from. All connections eventually come and go, and so when we tie our pleasure to other people, we cede influence over our feeling of joy to something external and transient.

According to certified therapist Alyssa Mancao, LCSW, the belief that our pleasure relies on something outside of ourselves is known as emotional reliance. "It is when our thoughts and self-worth are depending on external variables such as how another person feels about us.

The opposing side of the coin—and the aim, according to Mancao—is emotional independence. "People who exhibit emotional independence can build a feeling of contentment and tranquility despite what may be occurring in their life and relationships. This is not to suggest that they are never influenced by things that happen outside of them, but they still have a sense of who they are and can satisfy their own needs inwardly," she continues.

« **Being alone without friends.**

Being alone just implies you are physically by yourself—but it doesn't always mean you are lonely, which refers to a certain form of discomfort produced by the sensation that you're missing the companions and interactions you need.

While it's crucial to be able to appreciate being alone, we also need to have meaningful interactions in our lives—including friends, family members, a wider community, co-workers, and/or romantic partners. "Even real introverts tend to flourish when they have a particular someone (or two) to bond with," adds Manly.

Humans are social beings. We're naturally attracted to the community and crave interpersonal connection, in part because it's vital for our health and survival. "Loneliness and isolation may aggravate physical discomfort, depression, and immunity," a psychiatrist earlier noted that

"It raises the risk of diseases1 such infections, heart disease, high blood pressure, and dementia."

In other words, our well-being originates from a good balance of both togetherness and solitude—interdependence, as it's frequently called. So, if you're feeling lonely because you're truly missing a meaningful connection, learning how to be happy alone might help, but forming new connections may be just as vital.

»Being alone without a mate.

Many of us live in a society that hyper-focuses on romantic relationships as the primary and most essential way to interact with people, and in that setting, being single may seem like a curse whereby you're condemned to be lonely and sad until you can find yourself a mate.

In truth, there are so many opportunities to experience connection, closeness, caring, and love with people outside of simply sexual partnerships. Deep friendships, family ties, professional and creative collaborations, and interacting with a broader community may all be sources of meaningful connection with people if we open our hearts to it.

There are certainly numerous perks to being single that are less available inside the confines of a partnership. "When you are single, you are empowered to make your own decisions and hold yourself responsible for those choices," psychotherapist and relationship specialist stated "You learn to create your route, and it raises inner confidence and resilience." Being alone may genuinely be a great stimulus for personal development if we're prepared to truly interact with our loneliness rather than continuously seeking to escape from it.

»Being alone at home.

If you're living alone or in a period when you're home alone frequently, you may find yourself feeling lonely more often or in a more dramatic manner—perhaps in a way that shocks you. Some evidence shows individuals who live alone may be more prone to battle with mental health concerns, mostly originating from loneliness. No matter how independent you are, being alone at home will make most individuals feel a little lonely at least sometimes, and it's OK to identify these emotions. According to a holistic therapist, "the key is finding out how to reframe the way you're thinking about your alone time at home.

"Living alone, particularly whether it's for the first time or even after a transition, can be a highly emotional experience," she said, "There may be emotions of melancholy or loneliness, but living alone may also be a time of learning to appreciate yourself."

Know that many individuals choose to live alone on purpose because they sincerely like their isolation, and with time and a bit of a viewpoint adjustment, you may grow to feel less lonely in your circumstance too—and even learn to love it.

CHAPTER 2

»11 STEPS TO BE HAPPY ALONE

1. Don't push it.

First and foremost, go easy on yourself here. Everyone suffers loneliness from time to time, and that feeling—like all feelings—is entirely legitimate. "Humans are inherently social animals, so it's vital to remember that you're not 'broken' if you tend to feel a bit blue when you're alone," adds Manly.

Some individuals are also more inclined to companionship than others are, she points out, so be sympathetic with yourself if you're someone who just loves the company of others more frequently than not. "You're less likely to be plunged into despair if you don't anticipate yourself to have a high happy set point while you're alone," she adds. "By normalizing that many individuals feel less pleased when they're alone, you remove the responsibility off yourself to make yourself happy."

2. Keep yourself engaged.

When we're sitting around doing nothing, we tend to experience loneliness more strongly. "Time tends to slow down when we don't have plans," Manly continues, "so you're considerably more likely to be pleased when you don't have large periods of vacant time." She encourages preparing for alone time in advance, whether you know you have a lovely weekend coming up, you recently went through a breakup, or you're relocating to a new city by yourself.

"Make ahead arrangements to occupy the time in pleasurable ways," she suggests. "It's frequently nice to construct a list packed with a combination of must-do things and self-care time. This technique makes solitary days seem like a healthful mix of 'things you must do, and 'want-do-to- do's.'"

3. Fill your time with activities you truly like.

Alone time becomes a lot more tempting when we relate it with getting to do activities we enjoy and want to accomplish. For example, if you've always desired to read more, including a daily reading habit into your windows of alone time. If you're a skincare aficionado, treat yourself to a lengthy, sumptuous, and indulgent nightly skincare ritual.

When you fill your time with things that truly offer you joy, you change alone time from a moment of lack that you're having to suffer through into a moment of opportunity that you're delighted to embrace. "Strive to consider alone time as the ideal occasion to enjoy catching up on self-work, meditating, or sifting through piles of unread periodicals," adds Manly. "When we redefine solitary time in positive ways, the body, mind, and soul automatically begin to feel happier."

« Fun things to do alone.

1. Establish a workout program you enjoy and stick to it.

2. Carve out a particular time for reading in your daily or weekly agenda.

3. Start a garden (window gardens count!).

4. Practice applying your makeup.

5. Experiment with complicated hairstyles.

6. Buy a gaming system and play some video games.

7. Listen to podcasts while performing activities around the home.

8. Learn a creative pastime, like painting, cross-stitching, or writing fiction.

9. Get very excellent at anything practical, like cooking, web design, or investment.

10. Visit a museum or art gallery.

11. Take walks (or hikes!) frequently.

12. Play your favorite music on repeat.

13. Blast your favorite "guilty pleasure" tracks at maximum volume.

14. Learn a TikTok dance.

15. Explore your city (think farmers' markets, retail areas, cultural institutions) (think farmers' markets, shopping districts, or cultural sites).

16. Create a vision board.

17. Meditate every day.

18. Get highly informed about a specific field, like horticulture, organizational psychology, the MBTI, or anything else you're bizarrely interested in.

19. Learn to prepare some sophisticated foods.

20. Develop an exceedingly luxurious morning or evening habit.
21. Foster a pet.

4. Start a project.

In addition to pleasure activities, try digging into initiatives you've been wanting to start—such as beautifying the home, launching a community effort, or finally beginning that YouTube channel. Projects are fantastic ways to spend your time alone because they provide you with a purpose to strive toward and a means to occupy your time that feels significant.

"I have discovered, both myself and my clients, that being fully immersed in a creative pursuit may go a long way toward ameliorating loneliness," a psychology specialist remarked. "There is something about being completely immersed in the creative process that fills the heart and spirit with joy—even when we are working alone."

5. Take a social media break.

While social media might help us connect with others, research reveals that spending a lengthy time on social media can aggravate feelings of loneliness as well as reduce self-esteem. That's in part because social media frequently leads to unhealthy comparison, whereby we compare ourselves to what others are doing, what others have, and the social lives of others. So, try not to spend too much of your time alone reading through the applications, since it's likely to make you feel worse.

6. Reach out to friends.

Remember, being happy alone does not imply forgoing all social connections—quite the contrary, feeling close to people is crucial to our well-being, and if you're suffering loneliness in your life in general, it may be tougher to enjoy your alone time. "Although we want to be comfortable with our alone, it is also beneficial to connect with your support system, "Stay connected with those who offer you pleasure and encourage you."

The surest way to feel less lonely is to connect with people and develop those connections. That can involve ringing up your mom more regularly and developing your bond with her, or asking an old buddy whether they'd like to grab supper. Or, maybe it's time for you to look into creating new pals.

7. Engage with your community.

An oft-overlooked approach to interacting with people is via the community. Think reading clubs, yoga classes, local advocacy organizations, jogging groups, religious groups, and other communal places. Not only may these be venues for you to engage in new interests and ideas, but they're places where you can do so with other people and develop a feeling of shared belonging.

8. Establish routines.

"It's normal that loneliness peaks in the morning and at night when we don't have anything going on,". So, concentrate on building a good morning and evening routine that helps you flow through these sections of your day with greater comfort. "This may be a 10- to 15-minute exercise such as meditation, prayer, stretching, or a yoga flow," she explains. "Getting ready may also increase your attitude and help build a pleasant mental space to confront the day."

9. Get outdoors.

Remember that loneliness is a sensation that's typically an extension of the emotion of melancholy. That's why Manly advises walking as a possible remedy for loneliness. Walking comes with a plethora of mental health advantages (plus if it's out in nature, but any stroll will do!), with the mood being one of them. "Get outdoors for a little sunlight and exercise," she suggests. "Even if you take a short stroll, research suggests that there are lots of mood-boosting effects when we walk, soak up a little of nature, or just appreciate the sun's rays peeping through the clouds."

10. Mind your health.

By the same token, remember that our mood—that is, our emotional and mental health—is closely related to our physical health. How we treat our body influences how we feel emotionally, and vice versa. Manly observes that individuals who are coping with loneliness might often turn to harmful behaviors that simply compound the problem—for example, consuming foods that make you feel sluggish or losing out on crucial sleep that leads to anger and lack of energy, or being unduly sedentary.

"When we reframe solitary time to imagine it as the ideal chance to indulge in fantastic self-care—including filling up on tasty, wholesome food—we naturally feel happier and more balanced," she adds.

11. Work on your connection to yourself.

Perhaps most significantly, knowing how to be happy alone needs you to truly, legitimately love yourself. That implies you honestly like your own company, you care about your personal development and progress, and you genuinely find value in putting time and energy into the things that nourish you—the same way you find value in investing in your interactions with others.

If this isn't ringing true for you, start there. Maybe it's about learning how to create confidence in yourself. Maybe it's about relinquishing people-pleasing behavior. Maybe it's about surrendering perfectionism tendencies that lead to self-hatred. Maybe it's about implementing more positive affirmations into your life. Or maybe it's just about understanding how your connection with yourself may offer just as much joy, closeness, love, and support as your relationship with others.

Mancao proposes a thought-provoking technique to begin to practice this self-validation: "The next time you are seeking affirmation from someone else, ask yourself, 'What is it that I would want to hear from this person?' Then try speaking those words to yourself."

CHAPTER 3

« THE OUTCOME OF BEING SOLITUDE

People may experience real, true satisfaction in their alone. While we do need interpersonal connection in our lives in some form, it's very much possible to enjoy and even thrive living life as an independent individual rather than in a romantic partnership or living with others. In essence, learning how to be happy alone is about redefining how we think about our alone time—and how we think about ourselves.

highly vital for individuals to be able to source pleasure from the inside rather than depending entirely on the presence of others to obtain good sensations. Because all humans, unavoidably, will be alone occasionally. Yet, people are inherently social beings, and studies reveal interpersonal connection—whether in the form of friendships, family, professional and creative collaborations, community participation, or romantic relationships—is crucial to general well-being. So, genuine pleasure comes from a balance between enjoying your own company while also engaging with others in a nutritious manner.

Everyone will feel lonely from time to time, therefore it's necessary first to learn acceptance of these sensations as they show up. Once you can realize that loneliness is only a transient experience, it might seem less dire—and you can start working toward methods to feel more entire as well as more connected to people.

Alleviating feelings of loneliness starts with finding ways to truly enjoy your own company, whether that means developing peaceful morning and evening routines, embarking on a personal project or hobby that excites you, or deepening your relationship with yourself and your self-worth. Additionally, find methods to engage with people more often. Reach out to an old buddy and arrange plans. Ask that co-worker to coffee. Join a community sports team or club. Start a book club.

www.ingramcontent.com/pod-product-compliance
Lightning Source LLC
LaVergne TN
LVHW052115160826
845678LV00015B/3571

* 9 7 9 8 3 7 3 6 3 7 2 6 8 *